AMA*Zen*

LyricL Nkechi

Published in 2017 by FeedARead.com Publishing

A CIP catalogue record for this title is available from the British Library.

Art Work :   LyricL (Accessories, Stylist – Abia State, Nigeria)

Front: Samantha Jane (Fashion Designer – 'United80'
                  Brixton, London)

Back Cover: Bunny Bread (Artist - Image + Back Ink Design
                  'JazzReFreshed' London)

CONTENTS:

...Zen

Amazed

About The Author
Acknowledgements

Had an emotional, exceptional, excitable and eventful time compiling this. Step by step reminders that everything is relative. I shine cos 'we' shine. The vibrant flame that you see in our coldest and darkest hour brings forth both light and warmth – and does so selflessly!

Thank you oh so very much for your continued support and creative inspiration. I am truly humbled by your interest, blessed by the experience, honored by your consistency and beyond thankful for the opportunity in sharing my journey with you.

Through me, delivered to you and curated for us.

AmaZEN

Do what you love
Love what you do
...& Do Love!

LyricL

AMA*Zen*
= **Amazed** with **Zen**

AMA*Zen* is a book birthed from the impeccable debut offering entitled "Amazed", by lyricist, teacher and the BEFFTA spoken word/poet award winner, LyricL.

An effect of wonder and tender in words and verses.

This anthology, chronicles her troubadour journey to a life of zen.

A creative pool to the ripple of expressive, inspirational and perception writings in song, lyrics and poetry.

'APPRESHELOVED'

"Let your core be the chore that speaks through the chords."

Feeling both delicate and diligent at the moment.
Cannot put it into words
...Yet I cannot stop...

Especially when changes are positive and powerful.

All I can say is please please please please stay connected!

Let those you care for and hold dear know exactly that.

Let those you love romantically or otherwise, know that they are in your heart.

Let those who are in your good thoughts know you were thinking about them.

Let those you appreciate just for checking in on you on an ad hoc basis, know that you too are likely plus happy to do the very same!

Some people live alone

Some people feel alone

Some people are alone.

We are connected.

Through different ways,
...artistically,
...spiritually,
...creatively,
...socially,
...culturally,

7

…lovingly,
…memorably,
…beautifully all wonderfully!

When you lose something you panic or worry, then blame yourself whilst tracing your steps.

When you lose the love, in or for someone...I guess it's more of the same, except that feeling is far worse.

When you think you have or love, and then it is taken. (not misplaced or relocated or even in matters of the heart where the relationship is different), but gone...gone...gone, You are suddenly left looking at all the things you did, created, built, made or and appreciated about them,

...More so when you no longer have access to their very special light. Right?

Write.

Write a card - a letter - a poem - an email - a text - send it - send them - send flowers - go for a chai - go with chocolate - go with chicken - watch a comedy - watch a movie - watch a play – and play - play music - share music - share quotes - read an excerpt - read a proverb - read their eyes....please?

Even if tomorrow was promised.
What are you gonna do…

Today...?

'RUN AWAY'

We can just run away
We can just run away
Breathing in our own space

We can just run away
We can just run away
Living in a new place

Run away (leave & be free!)
Run away (leave & be free!)

Running from me …
…Running to you,
Running out of suggestions, when I haven't got a clue of
what to do,
Where to go,
Run out patience take it slow,
Don't blow a fuse.
Refuse to run away from all the things I need to do.

Running from my fears,
I might be running with tears,
But I'll hit the ground running till that ish disappears!

Running twice as fast as before,
Doubling,
Staying grounded when it seems that all around me now is
crumbling.

Something's troubling,
Friendship's struggling,
Stumbling on negative perspectives like a Goblin now
everythings a problem!

Running the risk of losing focus,

9

(of what's real and the feels the closest, from the bogus
things that nearly broke us!)

Kate Bush "Running Up That Road' …that hill,"
At my own will,
… Except a little further still.

Hoping that life reveals the answers,
Centred Chi Masters,
…far from disasters,
… plus my heart rate is much faster cos I'm running

Running!

We can just run away
We can just run away
Breathing in our own space

We can just run away
We can just run away
Living in a new place

Run away (leave & be free!)
Run away (leave & be free!)

'TRANSITIONING'

Bah-Bah Bah-Bah-Bah
…. Bah-Bah-Bah-Bah
Bah-Bah Bah-Bah Badoondaaay

Bah-Bah Bah-Bah-Bah
…. Bah-Bah-Bah-Bah
Bah-Bah Bah-Bah Badoondaaay – Transitioning

Transitioninnnnng

They did, We do, You arrrrrrrrrrrrrrrrrrre!
They did, We do, You are,
…Transitioning

They did, We do, You arrrrrrrrrrrrrrrrrrre!
They did, We do, You are
…Transitioning

Shifting moving, swiftly moving, embracing what we call
the new page.

A new direction, surreal perfection, the new progression
onto the next stage

Assimilating, gravitating, incorporating this new change.

Adaptation, Reorientation, elevation to the new phase.

Facing your fears, not wasting the years, tasting my tears,
running it's due course.

Kinda ashamed to say, I was afraid the day, faced up an
opening of new doors,
I didn't even realize, real time, what my life required
(surprise), can't ignore.

Embracing the journey, hearts yearn, heads turn from where
we once were before…

…Without getting too complex, passing from one state to the
next is oh so perfect.

Cannot really lose what's innate, when it's served on a plate
(guess you're just eating late?) …ah mate…wait!

Gonna hit and miss this, forever on my wish list
(…uh uh, but can I get a witness?)

Bah-Bah Bah-Bah-Bah
…. Bah-Bah-Bah-Bah
Bah-Bah Bah-Bah Badoondaaay – Transitioning

Transitioning

They did, We do, You arrrrrrrrrrrrrrrrrrrre!
They did, We do, You are… Transitioning

From a child,
To a girly-girl girl,
Adolescence,
Lady,
…Wooooman

Feel insecure?
Or somewhat confused?
…When embracing the new,
Sharing our truths.

Press down on the notes, (the notes)
You're now creating the chord-chords,
changing the key …

…We are transitioning
…We are transitioning.

See me coming through this,
Watching how we do this,
Notice how we move with ease.

…We are transitioning.

See me coming through this,
Watching how we do this,
Notice how we move with ease.

…We are transitioning.

See me coming through this,
Watching how we do this,
Notice how we move with eeeeeeease!

Bah-Bah Bah-Bah-Bah
…. Bah-Bah-Bah-Bah
Bah-Bah Bah-Bah Badoondaaay

Bah-Bah Bah-Bah-Bah
…. Bah-Bah-Bah-Bah
Bah-Bah Bah-Bah Badoondaaay – Transitioning

'KITE'

(Wow! … and I mean wow!
You know what's actually funny is I didn't even know I was
looking or…
Searching or even trying to find myself…
But I now know who I am …I know who I am now
…I am Freedom)

I am a kite, gliding through life,
I am freedom, in flight.
I am a kite, all turquoise and white,
Release me, at night.

I am a kite, gliding through life,
My name is freedom.
Ascending through heights,
Glistening bright.

I am the light. I am the light.

My name is Freedom. Freedom.
Delight,
Glistening,
Heights,
Bright,
The Light…
Right? Yeah….cos I know who I am now!

…know who I am…now..
My name is …. (freedom) freedom.

What I am, what I feel and who I am is..
…. (freedom) freedom.

I'm floating and flying, trying to sail taking dreams on my
journey to (freedom) freedom.

Turning and spinning, beginning adventures we venture to islands, places universal faces, it amazes my senses intensely focusing noticing all clouds minty blue fresh cool, beauty and zest my quest for…freedom.

I am a kite, gliding through life,
I am freedom, in flight.
I am a kite, all turquoise and white,
Release me, at night.

I am a kite, gliding through life,
My name is freedom.
Ascending through heights,
Glistening bright.

I am the light. I am the light.

It suits me when dreaming eyes closed from the roads And city, plus people all around us.
You'll find us each - season
Yet still with - reason …such freedom and wonderment, just ….flying …flying

Colours and shapes as my subtle self shakes,
To the rhythm of whistling winds.
Freshly cool blue,
Watching the sunshine through,
Hearing birds past my left and right….asking …

"Who are you…?" (My name is freedom)
"Who are you…?" (My name is freedom)
"Who are you?" (My name is freedom)
"Say it louder?"

My name is frrrreeeeeeedom!

I told you!

Trying to hold you,
I told you my mission,
Permission to float over oceans or moats with boats Over
people over places over all
…it's why… I
Love to …
Fly
(I love to fly!)

I'm trying to hold you,
I told you my mission,
Permission to float over oceans or moats with boats Over
people over places over all
… it's why… I love to fly.

I love to
Fly (I love to fly!)

Love – Fly

Love – High. (Love – Fly)
Love – High. (Love – Fly)
Love to fly.

Love …
Fly!

It's a good feeling, such a good good feeling,
In fact,
Such a great feeling!
Such a warm-warm, such a smooth-touch,
Sponge like soft, new,
Original skin, awake to the freedom.

Over oceans and seas, all alone – That's me!
…Feeling free, floating by - feeling light.
Passing treetop leaves, to the breeze,

All at ease, see me gliding whilst smiling in flight at my freedom.

In the moonlight of stars with sunset visions afar,
Twisting and turning in my own magical way.
Brightly coloured and shaped
…I continue to wriggle in order to
…Figure this out.

Release me like pigeon with messages,
The lesson is just as important as the learning,

Turning,
Rotating,
Weightlessness and yes,

I know who I am now.
My name is …. freedom

Freedom.

'EXPECTED TO DO SOMETHING'

I didn't really know that I,
I didn't really know that I,
....was expected to do something for you?

I didn't really know that I
I didn't really know that I
....was expected to do something for you?

I'm feeling cold and slightly shook / From all the things you overlook
Are my tears filling your void? / Does my truth make you annoyed?

As the injustice increases / Why are my people decreasing?
Your history repeating, / Such loudness, (how you sleeping?)

Please hear my truth and feel my song / Together tight, one fist, be strong./ To show us all the right from wrong / (Soon Mother Nature will respond!)

World Class 'Humanitarian?' / Live, Worlds and Walls you're tearing them!

Years after plots to bury them / Our children cry.
(Stop scaring them!)

Something that we should all expect, / The basic levels of Respect. /

All that you give, is what you'll get ...back
(Not to be taken as a threat that)

Someday you'll leave it all behind / You'll run to rule, then run to hide! /
You clearly know, yet think we're blind.

(Behind finance corrupted bribes!).All calculated far from wisdom / Our minds, also our Kings imprisoned. /
That fateful day, (Astro collision) / Karma will make fate your decision!

Perpetuate, (you're too persistent) / Such hatred ain't Police resistance. /
The way you ignore our existence. / The disrespect is too consistent. /

The things we do, just to be free / consistently from what we see /
To coexists a tragedy, / To know real love,
(why can't it be?)

You play too much, so now we act! / The final scene leaves all intact /
My truth is a matter of fact / Our Spirits cannot break or snap

…& that's that!

(in case you really didn't know)

I didn't really know that I,
I didn't really know that I,
….was expected to do something for you?

I didn't really know that I
I didn't really know that I
….was expected to do something for you?

The liberties you take,
Cloak and dagger snake-like personality,
Just for clarity,
… s not alright with me!

Everything! Everything you do, I see right through. Away from you I hold my space. A poison bitter taste of hate (and that's not great,)
…it's real.

Nourished.

Encouraged

Eat my words like a meal,
… Time to now reveal,
The way we feel without exception.

Your perception of me will never be my concern
Expectation is how to learn
…it's better the devil you know,
Though you cleverly throw …shade,
…grenades,
…mass graves
…just to bury the hatchet.

Cos you're okay with that sh*t?

You're okay with a lot of things,
You'll decay in a lot of Spring Seasons , (with reason)

Looking around for people pleasers,
… Misleaders,
… Deceivers,

Leaving you all alone and not leading you safely home.

Like bleeding through a Stone and just so know
…I was there!

I was there when people scattered,
…Lives shattered,
… Blood splattered and you were flattered that it really mattered?

Contrary to popular belief, I'm now at ease.

Everything is relative,
...Quantifiable,
...Undeniably true.

That I have nothing left for you.
(in case you didn't know)

I didn't really know that I,
I didn't really know that I,
....was expected to do something for you?

I didn't really know that I
I didn't really know that I
....was expected to do something for you?

I didn't really know that I,
I didn't really know that I,
....was expected to do something for you?

I didn't really know that I
I didn't really know that I
....was expected
... To do
... Something for youuuu!?

'HOPEFUL'

So woeful,
Plus vocal.
How do we live at your disposal?

I've seen it,
You've been it,
The answers we need are so revealing

No?

Not social,
It's global.
Your proposal is to be more noble,

Yes!

I'm coping,
and hoping

…it's okay.

Much more than negligence,
Hard working diligent, immigrant exodus.

Sipping on tea whilst you sit comfortably as you see the
unpleasantness all up close there in your 'tele-vijjjjshhh'

The fountain of youth, that is drowning the proof of the
truth is intelligence.
My sentence states, that the melodramatics we see,
…that's so tragically shown is all Melanin relevant.

Watching the media,
Shift was immediate,
(Felt like an eedieet)

That feeling of helplessness,
Needing more selflessness,
Seeing such selfishness,
All in a room full of elephants!

Don't take this as cockiness,
Drop the ball sloppiness,
Or somewhat shoddiness,
Ugliness breathes what the people believe,
To clear up all this fogginess we need more Godliness
...Now!

So woeful,
Plus vocal.
How do we live at your disposal?

I've seen it,
You've been it,
The answers we need are so revealing

No?

Not social,
It's global.
Your proposal is to be more noble.

Yes!

I'm coping,
plus hoping,

...it's okay.

More love interlinking,
Less logical thinking,
The right brain is shrinking,
...on days my hearts sinking,
Your kids are my children,
We walk on a pilgrim,

A plea for new thinking,
My third is unblinking,
Love still interlinking.
Yes! Logical thinking!
The right brain's still shrinking,
(Some days my hearts sinking)
Your kids are my children!
(Re-walk on a pilgrim)
…A plea for new thinking is Now!

Thinking is Now
Thinking is Now

So woeful,
Plus vocal.
How do we live at your disposal?

I've seen it,
You've been it,
The answers we need are so revealing No?

Not social,
It's global.
Your proposal is to be more noble. Yes!

I'm coping,
plus hoping

…it's okay.

'OVERRIDE'

The world and everything,
is seated,
On your shoulders

But we can deal with it
Because we're wiser

…And much older.

It's refreshing just to see and hear you smile.

Although it took a while my child…

Each day… is better than before

I see you struggling so come and take my hand.
I see you struggling because I understand your pain.
I see you struggling because I understand
But we can override and fly!

I see you struggling so come and take my hand.
I see you struggling because I understand your pain.
I see you struggling because I understand
But we can override and fly
…Away

Not a single tear,
My dear,
Has been shed in vain.

No pain,
No suffering,
It's comforting,
'cos we can win!

Your dreams
Conceivable.

Believable.
Achievable!

Stand tall
Amongst the stars

Believe in you,
Be who you are!

I see you struggling so come and take my hand.
I see you struggling because I understand your pain.
I see you struggling because I understand
But we can override and fly!

I see you struggling so come and take my hand.
I see you struggling because I understand your pain.
I see you struggling because I understand
But we can override and fly
...Away

'GARDEN OF PEACE'

I, I, I
I, I, I
Miss running through the garden with you … you

I, I, I
I, I, I
Miss running through the garden with you … you

See you glistening
So bright, day light.

All our people listening
Tonight your mine.

We be blossoming,
Friendship close knit.

People gossiping,
Too soon that's it!

We were planting seeds,
To grow and show,

Counting fallen leaves,
My dreams - don't go

I, I, I
I, I, I
Miss running through the garden with you … you

I, I, I
I, I, I
Miss running through the garden with you … you

See the morning dew,

Catch me, if I fall,
Now we mourning you,
Can't be…? Please call!

I'm waiting here,
Rooted – Fruitful.

Hearts breaking here!
Truthful.
Neutral.

I shake my head,
One rose, eyes close
Placed down on the flower bed,
…Don't gooooo!

I, I, I
I, I, I
Miss running through the garden with you … you

I, I, I
I, I, I
Miss running through the garden with you … you

So beautiful.
Sunrise sunset
Yes it's doable.
Stay close, silhouette
Cultivated sacred grove,
Evergreen, wilderness.

I'm feeling it! Seeing it! Heeling in!
Garden of Peace…
Garden of Peace…
Garden of Peace.

'BATTLE AND HARM-ONY'

It's like a tidal wave / Same final stage / engraving paving stones, / hand prints, near Brad Pitt, that's it? / Red carpets no new steps, / yet few rep'resent with intent, / price of life, no strife, (money well spent) / not lost, at what cost? The bridge we now cross, is called choice / Throwing rolls on Rolls Royce's plus Bentleys a'plenty / Teach kids to have no voice and be empty not mindful, (so spiteful!) /

Although that wasn't your journey / living that life, you can decide what their learning! / World turning on its axis / fact is, we're planet sharer's, (habitual non carers!) / It scares us, (scares me), they're not free!

Can't breathe / Disease! Like a swarm of bees with VD & TB (without jabs) / On these streets they meet stabs and bullets / red hot damned in Pudding Lane, so explain? / To those you thought wouldn't, / folks who couldn't, age groups that shouldn't... then reset.

Candles and flowers down / Walk your pet. / Read tabloids on tablets and iPads, add fire to the liars / Void the truth to

29

raise fear / we cheer, increase the beer, toast and raise spirits / to numb the pain, as numbers change to real names, (it's insane!)

Food for thought, contained at the top of the food chain / The downpour with blood on the dance-floor / If "rhythm is a dancer" then who's playing? / "We ah go party hard hard.." to swallow your pride / The truth runs yet we can't cry. Why?

Matters what we hear, what you're saying! ...and why's everyone 'slaying'? / Why's this or that said to be 'dead?'/ And what right now is giving you 'life?' / Where this alleged 'tribe?' / ('cos I never read a single memo about a fight?!)

...Yet we know, "there's a war going on outside" / "battle me that's a sin", / The battle within. Asking contestants "what exactly do you win?" / And was it even worth it? / Facing filters, selfie picture perfect, / The circus where the entertainment is we / Re runs of the "The Running Man" on TV....no no no...it doesn't have to be!

....

Much harder when against the grain. / Prevent what's meant to maim, / "Wait in vain for your love." / It's real. What brings you joy now you must steal from your own thoughts and true dreams, / Sun beams, warm the hearts on like-minded teams.

Trusting yourself with whatever feels right, / Gaining insight, delights and new heights! / An end game and end goal, / A new role, the next show and tell, the fortune wheel will come again then set sail, (without fail!), / Without addictions or restrictions!

I'm saying this with conviction,
...To find the we
In all certainty,
It most certainly
...so must start
...with 'Me!'"
Battle and Harm-ony

'BLACKBIRD'

Transcendent.
Reverent.
Yes you shine in divine excellence!

Blackbird – mysterious – freedom - Lunar Sun,
Spiritual path embark and pass everyone!

So now is the time,
…Plus we see who you are,
Cannot wait,
…it's your fait,
Having faith - Be your star.

Must just trust in the richness of self.
The value of you, far beyond priceless wealth!
Magnitude of magnificence.
Togetherness, Intelligence.
Eternal. Wisdom and also benevolence.

Your extended wings,
How it brings vulnerability,
Reach possibilities,
Embracing serenity.

Heights – Spirit-guide, find your truths through dreams.
Your presence is felt – even when you're unseen!
Changes are happening,
Awakening minds.

So get up and get ready, fly
Leave it all behind.

Blackbird.

'CAN'T WAIT'

Can't wait to get to you
My heart beats to your melody
We harmonise with our eyes
I really can't wait to get to you

No valley low, river wide and further more there "Ain't No Mountain"
Patiently waiting no doubting, heart pounding my chocolate fountain You Sweet me!
Knowing you're waiting to meet me,
Hot Green-tea.
…Facewash with Tea-Tree, you please me!

More than considerate,

Our feelings are intimate,

Our love is deliberate,

Spiritually me-to-you-to-me forever infinite.

Speechless.
Uniqueness,
…My knees feel weakness,
(seams all my dreams have come true, because I sleep less.)

Bless

Yes it's so funny our connection,
If "music be the food of love", you are my rhythm section.
Picture perfection.

Reflective bass to my heartbeat.
Partly because you'll never dark me.
Your love it tends to spark me…I'm glistening!

Listening to our souls flying.
When you're not around if I don't miss you, then I'm lying.

(I'm trying to let you know my feelings)
I'm here when I'm next to you,
I'll never ever be an ex to you.

And can't wait to get next to you.

… I can't wait!

Can't wait to get to you
My heart beats to your melody
We harmonise with our eyes
I really can't wait to get to you.

Can't wait to get to you
My heart beats to your melody
We harmonise with our eyes
I really can't wait to get to you

'KNOW YOU'

I guess I really want to know you.
I … I really want to
…know (oh-oh-oh)
I just
….wanna know!

Wanna know

Wanna know

You you yoooooou!

Passing double glances – 'dimpled grins' begins our initial
encounter.

Looking down an elongated swan smooth posture.
(I lost your attention for a split second), your friend
beckoned - I recognized the exuberance – although fairly
new to this…I wave.

Saved the embarrassment, as my out stretched arm,
followed a fake 'yawn',
…was how the moment was torn…

…away.

You stay.

Eyes widen in shocked we lock consciousness.

Yes I messed up,
Pushed buttons,
No rewind,
(must be outta my head!)

Mislead, sign read 'no entry'

its not what I meant – see,

Time-out - now benched
Me,

In the lurch.

Perched bar-side, ginger beer - throwing tear salted cashews,
at you,

I chew my unsaid, unheard murmured words, (it mattered),

Scattered like birdseed, my heart bleeds as I watch you
leave.

… Take a few steps, then…

Stop,
Turn,
Look,

I'm shook like train tracks, (option to inhale comes back –
short),

"oh I thought you were gonna say something,?'
"aah ha" (awkward laugh),
"aah haa!" (think the second one was the worst!)

Coerced to pay my dues - got reimbursed - nursing my
wounds in shame,

You ask me for my name. "…err Lillian"
(million reasons why I shared that truth!)

A new sign where 'trust' meets 'proof', with nothing to lose,
now boosts a large spoon fed smile.
A shapely mouth warms hearts and cools doubt.

A light goes out.

Yet neither of us turn.

…Although at that very moment we both learn,

Something new

And special.

This me
…and you.

Wanna know.

I guess I really want to know you.
I … I really want to
…know (oh-oh-oh)
I just
….wanna know!

Wanna know

Wanna know

You you yoooooou!

'ELEPHANT'

Powered up to cower down the other day,
(I know right?)
All tall talented, smart, sexy, suave 'whoaaah',
Lets see ahhhh 'creatively'
…basically

Cornered!

Crying.

Lying fetus shaped. Thinking faeces wait. Small bits of peace
then hate. A loving giving living species fate,
(Can't articulate) Yet these things happen…wait
… why?

Lifestyle preferential.
Fear differential.
Tears…
Torrentially…
Down

…pour.

So appalled.
Ignoring faith restoring measures.
Severed.
Dismembered by the heartfelt priceless things once
treasured.
Together.
That right now, I just can't even remember
…any.

(It's hard!)

The blatant disregarded. Scars no one notices.
My blood crawls, locusts, roaches.

Ever lasting tattoos of condolences,

(What's the prognosis when you know that this is more than enough!)

Elated…
…and now … devastated.

Suffocated.

Drawing breath through short straws.
Constricted.
Restricted.

Fresh air-ing words from conflicting sides,

With one inflicting lies,
…and the other's airtight eye cries that don't count as truth,
(unless you're bulletproof!)

Blacked out!

Blacks … doubt …things will improve,
…'cos what hurts deep trust must hurt you?

Loathing the fact you're so specific,
As loved ones number your statistics!

Olympic flags tarnished.
TV coverage … carnage!

Horror film called 'Demographics.'
Something's got to give … semantics
Snap elastic stings, as Old Blue Eyes sings that "Old Black Magic" this tragic World Stage brings.

Scissor sit-ups cuts into the abs …
Double jabs. Psychological stabs.
The lies, fibs, rib crunches …punches afternoon lunch is

... disgusting!

Revolting.

Insulting my intelligence,

Ikea flat-packing all your skeletons,

Decadence of evidence,

Consistency of pestilence,

The hash tag and my melanin,
Are all very much relevant,

...as to why

...right now,

...this room

...is full

...of

Elephants.

'TRY'

Don't you know that you
Don't you know that you

Got to
Keep on

Trying harder!

Don't you know that you
Don't you know that you

Got to
Keep on

Trying harder!

Try - Try - Try (tryyyyyy!)
Try - Try - Try - Try (Try tryyyyyy!)

As I'm making new decisions for myself I've surpassed,
Lift my chin, breathed in, walked away from the past.

Realization relocation, opportunities grasped.
(Guess you really set sail once you've centered your mast.)

The task was undertaken, overtaking with speed.
Only person really in this competition is me!

Everybody's very hungry
(Yes I know you'll agree),
Filled with greed,
Whilst others tend to either lead or mislead!

I can see that people daily try to free-up themselves,
Dig deep to seek the richness yet don't value the wealth.
Sick and tired of this treatment stop defeating yourself.

This inner attack,
(Reflecting on a mirror that's cracked!)

Running up and down the treadmill, still you keep looking back?

It's okay to make mistakes – but not to counterattack.

If the lesson keeps returning then decisions you lack,
Being comfortable or irresponsible isn't that,
That's a fact
...but keep trying!

Don't you know that you
Don't you know that you

Got to
Keep on

Trying harder!

Try - Try - Try (tryyyyyy!)
Try - Try - Try - Try (Try tryyyyyy!)

Course I knew "it's gonna work", cos you made it make sense,
Even those times it really hurt, yet still you made that attempt!
(Not even thinking about shoes, suit or money you spent,
Or the days you went berserk and barely making the rent!)

Heaven sent ...excellent... many blessings bestowed.
Prayed you'd catch a break and not the flu or a cold.

Said that 'you could stay',
Then all your clothes they now fold,

(...And everybody heard what happened yet your truth ain't been told)

… so be bold.

Say it loud. Over power the lies,
Who was answering your phone calls when you needed to
cry?

Toe to toe
Friend and foe with no one blinking an eye…
Quickly changing their tone as you're now shopping to buy,
a shop in Dubai, a car in Berlin. Your battle to win, life took a
spin,
(Oh what a funny situation you're in!)

What it is within your heart ah'beg believe and dream. Seek
…find
Even speak it 'til you succeed,
…but keep trying
So just try!

Don't you know that you
Don't you know that you

Got to
Keep on

Trying harder!

Try - Try - Try (tryyyyyy!)
Try - Try - Try (tryyyyyy!)

'ORANGES SO AREN'T ONLY...'

Maaaaaate!

A Pink Lady got just destroyed
I mean absolutely finished!
Grabbed
Picked Up
Got rinsed
Really wasn't necessary to get cut though,
... but yeah.. Gone? Just like nothing!

There were onlookers and everything.
I mean, people saw the whole thing... and didn't do or say anything.

(Hear it happens in certain parts of the world right, except where they don't have much, or choices, proper poor, or those poverty stricken areas yeah...but everywhere else... boiiiii, 5... a day!)

Situation came up where I myself actually got into one...(and to be fair from the time all the Pink Ladies got to my place, caught me on the wrong foot, I tripped, they now all start rolling in my kitchen being fresh and sh*t!)

Then stopped.

Me now, calm, checked bruses, looked up, then thought "fine, I see you innit" plus I knew what time it was with these ones, so understood from that day, being in my space and in my face, huh...was short term!

On the whole, you think or presume that people don't judge you. And what's really strange is how well these Pink Ladies are received as well as seen by people in general, I mean by all people, everyone...Vegans, Pescatarians, Vegetarians, Rastafarians, Bikers Hikers Hausas Hindus Horses, Rabbits,

Rabbis, Allies ah lie?...like everyone, accepts them...just as
they are.

You'll recognise them by their mixed yellowy red smooth
skin, freckled, (although their initial origins as well as all
their seeds are naturally dark and rooted)

It's just sad I suppose on occasions when they are
overlooked and just left to rot. How things change as well as
perceptions. Guess that's life...or perhaps
just
one
bad apple.

Thought about posting a picture of me actually eating one of
them but decided against it.

'WE CAN MAKE IT'

We Can

Make It!

Make moves
Make something happen
Make someone smile
Make yourself laugh...out loud!
Make something healthy & nice to eat it, after doing
something fun & active

Make that all important phone call you yourself hoped to
receive.

Make time for an elder
Make a difference in a child's life
Make a difference to the City you live in.
Make a promise (oh and make sure you can fulfill it!)

Make love
Make a poem...some art...a picture
Make a prayer ...or just make today memorable.

(None of these things are easy ... yet none are actually
impossible!)

*in truth, I was gonna say make Egusi Soup, Fish Tea or
Shepherds Pie with Sweet Potato, then thought, 'ohh c'mon
you've only just woke up!'*

...yet still...

We Can - Make It!

'WHEN YOU READ THIS'

When you read this...

Know you were on my mind, make me smile, are in my prayers, good thoughts, smothered by my love and permanently resident in my heart.

When you read this...

You won't remember when where or even how we connected the way we do, but the feeling you got from the connection is infinite real and ever present.

When you read this...

You will chuckle from a private joke, sigh from a sad memory as well as pause in appreciation of us as people... friends.

When you read this...

You will once again see something truly beautiful within yourself,

Experience a valuable moment of mystical spiritual awareness,

A desire to share this very pure, powerful, yet invisible thing and hold it dear.

Gasping yet grasping ever so tightly, just from the fear of its uniqueness getting lost in the mundane of everyday ... life.

But like you, that uniqueness is innate

...and great

...and glorious. It will always be tHERE...in hand...increasing the warmth, everytime you reach out toit, that light and also ... Sparkle!

When you read this...

You will frown and think about when we last connected,
kissed, hugged, laughed, loved, linked, listened ... spoke,
joked, toked ... trained, entertained ... give ... lived, fought,
caught, cuddled, huddled, danced, romanced, created,
waited, hated then felt elated ...all ... none ...or just one.

...as I personally pause respectfully,

... in silence,

Just to be thankful.

Reading the writing on the walls of stillness,

Learning more about you

...me

...everyone

...everything

...everyday

...and especially right now now,

...wondering

...about this very moment ...

... when you ...read 'this!

'LADYLIKE'

Head-over heals, diets, domestic,
Mother Nature, orgasms and lipstick,
Patience, yoga, you opening doors,
So stand up tall to applaud because you know
....its LadyLike ...ooooh its Ladylike...yeah!

Stance, face, elegance, grace, sophistication
Dance, waist, elephant, pace, menstruation
Inner strength, cow, intense,
...Submissive,
Intuition, queen, whore and then there's bitches!

Foot binding, strength, breast, identity,
High heels, Mother-Earth,
Sexuality - Ethnicity.

Persona, Salsera, Empress,
Spinster, B-Girl, Side-Chick, Wife, Feminist

Crossed legs.

Moon, Womb, Lesbian.
Panther, Bae, Queen, Breathe, Intelligence,

Open-legged

Manners, Crone-Feline, Hag,
Womanly, Beauty, Curves
...and handbags - shaved heads.

Botox, in-plants and Femidom
Clitoridectomy, silk, lace and tampons
Brazilian,
Queen-B, Black Widow Spider,
Aggressive, worldy, graceful inna your 'Batty-Rider'

Nurturing, African, accepting, flirtatious
Graceful, soft, naive, Amazon, actress

Ambitious, physically, imposing, hard,
Innocent, demanding, soft - security guard?

Same-Sex, weak, graceful, boxer, electric drill,
Cheerleader, parking, morning after pill
…and talking

Iron-Lady, Canilingus, Open Toe and Camel Toe
Ice-queen, Cat woman, Bag Lady, Childbirth and 'Ho!'

Head-over heals, diets, domestic,
Mother Nature, orgasms and lipstick,
Patience, yoga, you opening doors,
So stand up tall to applaud because you know
….its LadyLike
…ooooh its Ladylike…yeah!

Head-over heals, diets, domestic,
Mother Nature, orgasms and lipstick,
Patience, yoga, you opening doors,
So stand up tall to applaud because you know
….its LadyLike
…ooooh its Ladylike…yeah!

'TAKE'

We are rich, plus we are strong,
We're ambitious, we live long,

We have answers, we have schools
…plus a multitude of tools.

Culture, food, traditions, class,
Medicinal methods enhanced,

Theology, Power and Art
(we've had them all right from the start)

Togetherness
Faith, hand and glove,

Philosophies,
Spirit & Love
Family, Community (just how it always used to be!)

We congregate we celebrate
Continue to elevate.
They came from planets, land and seas
…yet can't take Africa from me!

'LIPS SYNC'

He read my lips,
I read his scripts.

He loves my voices,
I love his choices.

He loves my accent,
I love his actions!

Music speaks through us,
Creative nuance.

So love to dance,
…Plus always laugh!

Enlightened thirds,
Painting with words.

Flowering seeds,
Empowered dreams.

More to the eye than what it seemed
…this 'We!'"

'TRYING TIMES'

Trying...

Trying to reach out whilst heal through music words art and sound
Trying

Trying hard to not knee jerk sentences, digest the unjust injustices, from the unsaid, on those in need, indeed yes, I am …
Trying

Trying to keep pumping, sharing, growing my love through a big heartbroken heart, encapsulated and entrapped within a protective rib cage purpose built for angry Black Women…Trying

Trying to answer your initial 'how are you?' message without speaking up, feeling low, raising voices, whilst sending prayers high above, from this our poisonous planet below. Where silence is golden and its value as well as residence, depreciate at a rate, on special celebratory days or when onlookers both perpetuate and appreciate stary nights.

Glistening and allergically listening, in order to 'Rise 'n' Sh1te'…type o trying

Trying to see the nakedness of the Emperor without cringing at the truth, in an un-empowered, unimportant unimaginable way, but hay, I'm trying...

Trying

...crying...and yet still, trying

… Hard!

'FRUITS OF OUR LABOUR'

Tired of this waiting
It's a little bit frustrating
Why you hating on me right now…huh?

Tired of this waiting
It's a little bit frustrating
Why you hating on me right now…huh?

Tired of this waiting
It's a little bit frustrating
Why you hating on me right now…huh?

Tired of this waiting
It's a little bit frustrating
Why you hating on me right now…huh?

I'm working.

Working for you, working for me, plus working to be the best best

Working for us, if works not enough then how can we manifest this?

I'm working on me, just working to see the fruits of our labour,

If this doesn't work, and my heart gets hurt,
…We live and we learn… what was working.

If only there were more hours in the day, more heartfelt things to say, or even if you could see things slightly my way you know?
I even sacrifice sleeping, rearrange everything just to connect and meet him!
(What's this deep water that my feet's in?)

Problems - repeating - displeasing.
Dedicate a week also a weekend (we're important!)

Romantically courting. Sorting what to eat,
Where to go, what we're doing.
(Ahh sorry, no, next week I can't and now you're screwing?)

Doing my head-in, hamster peddling for a wedding? Sowing
the seeds, we proceed to lead the threading.

Happy Ever After? Love-laughter not Armageddon.
Don't know how to face this now, yet
wonder where it's heading...still ...working.

Working..

Working for you, working for me, plus working to be the
best best

Working for us, if works not enough then how can we
manifest this?

I'm working on me, just working to see the fruits of our
labour,

If this doesn't work, and my heart gets hurt,
...We live and we learn... what was working.

'BEEN SO LONG'

Been so long,
it's like the missing part is underrated,
No I'm not frustrated,
…but some days are great, whilst others are …

Not so…

…we're so,

…it's been so

… near - yet

…so far-away,

…my love's here to stay (you say!)

So so much, yet you're actions much louder.

Night times are colder,
…for me, I need a shoulder.

Heart wide open
…hoping you'd notice

Holding tight this closeness

…It's hopeless
… 'cos it's been

Sooo

…Long!

'ENIGMATIC'

When I read all the things you said,
It felt much more than words.
Any or everyone could see,
… but 'me'
My heart now stirred!
(that bit was not supposed to rhyme neither the other part)
…regardless yes I feel so blessed,
Two souls - our love - one heart.

Answers increasing at great speed,
No time to even question.
I hear you talking then we speak,
Connecting - no exceptions.

You touch your neck,
Then feel my hands,
Palms, fingertips and pulse,

Within that heat we hear our beat,
Something so far from false!

With you the anything is clear,
And 'everything' makes sense.
Residing inside, deep within,
Where beauty manifests.

Reflective and perfecting,
Daily routines life plus living.
It's still ok, that's just the way,
…because you are so giving.

My text …
Your phone…
Our human zone…
Ancestors all ascending…

Into the Universe together,
(Love that's never ending!)

I do get kinda freaked and when I do, it's not surprising.

Our love of lifetimes lived before
You're still here, right beside me!

And now it is y/our time to breathe
Uplift - shine - glow - be - fly!

You do not have to worry, (no),
Your you plus me makes 'I'

I hear you... See you.. Feel you...Know you as I know
myself.

The best things come to those who wait
...beyond Orion's Belt.

'FAR'

uuh uuh uuh ah-ah-ah,
uuh uuh uuh ah-ah-ah
uuh uuh uuh ah-ah-ah,
uuh uuh uuh ah-ah-ah

Why you so far? So far?
Why you sooooo …. faaaar?
Why you so far (from me?)
Far! Why you so (soooo soooo)
Faaaar? Why you so far? (soooo soooo)

Now I don't really see myself as demanding, Commanding
things that bring a swing in our axis,
The fact is 'I' wasn't ready.

A change is gonna come but I wanted you delivered,
I quiver at the thought of you being scared,
ill prepared on that journey from ….here to… …Somewhere
else, (all by yourself).
Locked boxed and shelved,
re-understanding life's wealth.

Words said (just before) I can no longer ignore,
The encoure replays and replays each day,
(with slightly longer delays),
I guess we're both in the next phase. I take to the stage.

Both on the same page but now that chapter is missing.
Torn. Forlorn. Opposing beauty of a new born.
Silent screams. Fractured dreams. Tear filled streams turn
into waves…crashing!

Patterns no longer matching…dismissing emotions as I stare
across oceans and seas just to see…to hope…to cope…but
nope. Nothing

Nothing.

Why you so far? So far?
Why you sooooo …. faaaar?
Why you so far (from me?)
Far! Why you so (soooo soooo)
Faaaar? Why you so far? (soooo soooo)

Its so import that…
uuh uuh uuh ah-ah-ah
That your memory
(lives…deep deep down it lives)
uuh uuh uuh ah-ah-ah
uuh uuh uuh ah-ah-ah

it lives
uuh uuh uuh ah-ah-ah
it lives
uuh uuh uuh ah-ah-ah

Its so import that…
uuh uuh uuh ah-ah-ah
That your memory
(lives…deep deep down it lives)
uuh uuh uuh ah-ah-ah
uuh uuh uuh ah-ah-ah

it lives
uuh uuh uuh ah-ah-ah
it lives
uuh uuh uuh ah-ah-ah

'CREATIVE HEALING'

Finding Strength through Writing.

Sharing Truth.
Singing - Poetry.

Taking trips away.
Stillness by the Sea.
Stillness by water.

Being alone with yourself.
Laughter with others.
Nature. Retreats.

Seeing.
Sights.
Scents.
Rose coloured glasses.
Reading and singing into the stories.

Breathing.

Meditation.

Faith.
Awake.
Alive.
Living.

Newness.
New home.
New city.
New relationship.
New love.
Loving again.

Waiting. Wanting.
Watching. Walking.
Running.
Riding bikes, horses, the wind.
Sailing.
Flying.
Playing.

Painting. Plaiting Hair - Cut.
Colour. Decor.

Decorate a house.
Gardening.
Growing. Grafting.
Carpentry. Shaping. Building.

Renewal.
Response.
Silence.
Stillness.
Substance.

Something.
Anything.
Everything.

No longer being afraid to try.
No longer being ashamed.
Saved.
Standing tall.
Confidence.
Telling y/our story.
Finding y/our voice.
Supersede.
Supervision.
Super Power.
Recognition.
Perspiration - Realization.

Seeing how far you've come!

Elevation.
Embracing life.
Acknowledgment.

Being Thankful - Doing what is needed of you to do,

....however long is has taken to do so

...and now

Arriving.

Right there
Right here.

...and that it's okay.

To just be.

Be present.
Encapsulated

At times going without - By going within.

Your Space.
Safe Space.
Sanctuary.
Synergy.
Harmony and Remedy...

....for Creative Healing.

'WANNA MAKE'

You
I wanna make everything with you-oo
I wanna make you
my …
everything…new…you

I wanna make sure that everything is okay.
I wanna bake bread - fresh towels - white pillows when you
stay.
Arrival lounge, with Marvel for flight delays.
Nice credit life – "it's alright - I'll pay!"

Check on your Ma say, "hay!"
Jallof, fish Moy-Moy served on a plate.

I wanna laugh when you're laughing,
Massage your calves in,
Even perv on you when you're bathing,
(I just wanna…)

Read books that you'll notice,
With in-depth talks - we quote that and quote this.
I wanna be there when you need me.
Pretend everything's cool - then you read me!

Walk for time on a summer's night,
Write new lines, spit tight rhymes and feel hype…I just
wanna show…
Real love that's serious,
Where we reflect both - real close, like mirrors …(ohh!)

Much bigger than marriage,
Manage all our flaws - Hilton - Paris.

Fine from behind (thank God when you're walking),
Kiss mouths talking - with no pork in …ah maaaate,

Staring not stalking (bait). Feels great,
Wait, I don't wanna temp fate...I kinda...
Really really wanna hug you,
(That WhatsApp green symbols yo is gonna bug you...You!)

You
I wanna make everything with you-oo
I wanna make you
my ...
everything...new...you

Wanna be... fully me when I represent,
And for you the intend to be excellent!
Wanna feel Spring 'hot-cool' reasons,
Hug trees fall and not leaf - seasons.

I wanna look into your eyes both glistening,
Appreciate time made - listening.
Lesson time where I learnt to, hold dear respect truth and
not hurt you!

Wanna feel legs give when you kiss me - frizbee spin,
Secret grin, "...aww babes, you gonna miss me aww?"
Be in synch with no clashes,
Spark like matches and sit down where your moustache is,
wow!
See what's happened to me now?...Applaud - high score,
Further more take a bow yessaai...
Wanna be your private dancer,
In fact, I wanna be the Universe's answer...to you!

You
I wanna make everything with you-oo
I wanna make you
my ...everything...new...you.

'HOW BEAUTIFUL'

Have eyes that speak volumes - talk of things you do.
Dedicated to change – Sincere - Living proof
Just making a difference, small steps with big heart.
Passionate and purposeful - eager to start
You're home late at night, yet the first to arise
Inspiring - innovative humble all smiles.
Things people won't discuss, you one open wide.
That nurturing nature, with pure love inside.

The city we work is the family you love.
The people you save, are commuters we shove.
Children that we teach, the young people we raise.
Are the infants you heal and teenagers you save!
I watch as you glide day to day – "what's in store?"
You're praying for Peace, yet for you, I want more!
So candid - kind hearted, the whole world I'd give
The things that you'd die for, it's time now to live!

When I'm standing with you - invincible tall.
You talk of these challenges - always on call.
("Please let me just love you. The world is as is")
I know I sound selfish but please don't forgive.

Today you must hear this, my words are my truth.
There's no one who loves you the way that I do!
For someone to save you and fight for your cause.
For blessings to bathe you – ("fortune open doors")
For you not to want and your needs always met.
For all your new tears to be happiness wet.
With your hand is on heart, looking upwards above.
No longer dismay, overwhelmed by pure love.
Regain faith in mankind as you've come so far.
That the world you still see, is how beautiful you are!

'WHY?'

(....Free...free in your mind, mental health it's the most
important! .. it's about finding that time, making that
time...you know? ....cos that's where the answers come. 'If
you don't go within, you go without!'...you've heard it
before, need to reiterate myself just to grab and grasp it
sometimes...why?)

Why?
Wont you ever find the time, to free your mind just.
Why? Wont you ever find the time, to free your mind...just
...Tryyyy
...to find the time, to free your mind oh!
Why...why whyyyyy!

Keeping quiet doesn't make it go away,
...with the choir does it mean you've got to pray,
...fighting does it means I'm led astray,
...riot so the people have a say with our voices and
choices...yet

I - have an impression that I'd kinda like to keep,
...lessons I'm learning every week,
...confession says that I'd really like to speak, a session
(without the weed?), we need stereotypical lyricals to now
proceed.

Getting - comfortable by what was done and did,
...we're responsible for everybody's kid,
...vegan's eating pig - wears a wig that is blonde, my
response to all the nonsense we miss, because of situations
like this?

Our - imprisonment is coming from the brain,
when overlooking everybody's pain or fate war-torn or
raped, kings and queen with low self-esteem who face
calculated hatred from patriots.

We'll - make it through the efforts of the heart,
(...or shake until the method falls apart),
...some express it through the heART,
Target practice poison dart, what was written from the start
can be changed rearrange once we ...

Quit from playing games, we'll succeed,
Stay the fighting lane with Godspeed,
Crying through the pain my throat screams, on dope beats it
don't mean, my votes are seen, or my hopes and dreams are
obscene.

The technical things they do from the food we consume.
The issues we're quick to perceive coming from the TV.
And as long as it's in all the papers then there's room for
hatred. I guess then it must be the truth if it was on the
news?

(...food we consume.)
(...from the TV)
(...our newspapers)
(...must be the truth!?)

Why?
Wont you ever find the time, to free your mind just.
Why? Wont you ever find the time, to free your
mind...just...Tryyyy
...to find the time, to free your mind oh!
Why...why whyyyyy!

'FIGHT IT'

Fight it. Fight it.
Because what's killing me, just has to be killing you too?
Fight it...ooh, fight it.
Taking without giving, yet we're forgiving your untruths.

Fight it. Fight it.
Because what's killing me, just has to be killing you too?
Fight it...ooh, fight it.
Taking without giving, yet we're forgiving your untruths.

Taking what you need out of greed we believed we were
equal.

Statistics and numbers you see, not family or people.

It's nice to be important, but more important to be nice.
Solidarity and transparency creates the up-rise

You're sleeping so soundly yet evil's surrounding your
whole Soul

I look all around me, where people are hungry and still cold.

This critical state is our fate not political statements
… The decision makers are fake and their promises
weightless!

Fight it. Fight it.
Because what's killing me, just has to be killing you too?
Fight it...ooh, fight it.
Taking without giving, yet we're forgiving your untruths.

Fight it. Fight it.
Because what's killing me, just has to be killing you too?
Fight it...ooh, fight it.
Taking without giving, yet we're forgiving your untruths.

'LIVE OUT LOUD'

Reaching for those dreams and live your life.
Things ain't what they seem so live your life.
Reaching for those dreams and live your life...
live out loud ...and-to-the full-est!

Reaching for those dreams and live your life.
Things ain't what they seem so live your life.
Reaching for those dreams and live your life...
live out loud ...and-to-the full-est!

Tomorrow isn't promised
As we ...
...shut our-eyes, we-open-up-to
Endless possibilities

Sunset-warmth refreshing blues re-new
Turning dreams into opportunities

Reaching for those dreams and live your life.
Things ain't what they seem so live your life.
Reaching for those dreams and live your life...
live out loud ...and-to-the full-est!

Forth & back-back forth - tennis courts – advantage
Take a lot of things for granted

Enhance our lives by the things we upgrade
Next stage, happy days we get paid!

Got it made.
High grade.
(Who's showing up?)
Hand grenades like wow 'pow' 'you blowing up?'
Growing up, 'til the clock stops - you did what?
You poor, helpless and selfness? (err nope, I think not!)

So why are you complaining about a life?
Watching the wrongs of this world
...but you don't write...right?

Call it as I see it, no it's not in spite,
I'm just a human - being...
...myself...just a little extra.
(Subservient plus a little vexed bruh?!)

Delight in our pleasures at all cost.
"But where's the light when you measure the Souls lost?"

Did you make someone smile,
Help someone's child or just profile?

Living for today, thinking of tomorrow.
Understanding sorrow just from someone's 'hello?'

Wanna break it down, well in all fairness,
You work hard - drop the ball (ah so careless?)

They tear us apart when they scare us,
But we're still here cos we're planet sharers!

...even on those days y when you feel a little weaker,
(da man dem or sexy chica),
Just thinking, "Yeah, I am I my brothers keeper!"
Until you feel real love coming through the speaker.

Reaching for those dreams and live your life.
Things ain't what they seem so live your life.
Reaching for those dreams and live your life...
live out loud ...and-to-the full-est!

'JUXTAPOSE'

It's just the position I'm in,
With all the decisions they bring...I'm
...just-kinda-wishing that things would be clearer

It's just the position I'm in,
With all the decisions they bring...I'm
...just-kinda-wishing that things would be clearer

Come nearer to meee...Just suppose?
Nearer to me - Juxtapose
Juxtapose-Juxtapose

Juxtapose

Together or next to, I'm not getting vexed, us comparing the
sexes is wrong.
It's amazing, life rearranging, seems to be changing
...So strong

He sees it, (well it isn't a thesis),
...though I'm guessing we need this right now.
Where's it going? Our love's growing,
Reap what we sow - but just how?

Cannot conceal it, way that I'm feeling, far more revealing,
(it's true!)
Overly zealous , your ex - jealous?
I still could care less , (what's new?)

Couple advances with difference stances,
"You see how I'm dancing with you?"
This moment is ours, connecting our powers,
...Heaven allow this break-through.

It's just the position I'm in,
With all the decisions they bring...I'm
72

…just-kinda-wishing that things would be clearer

It's just the position I'm in,
With all the decisions they bring…I'm
…just-kinda-wishing that things would be clearer

Come nearer to meee…Just suppose?
Nearer to me - Juxtapose
Juxtapose-Juxtapose

Juxtapose

'DAH-DOOM'

Dah-doom dah-doom-dah-doom day-du da doom day-du da da-doom

Dah-doom dah-doom-dah-doom day-du da doom day-du da da-doom

Dah-doom dah-doom-dah-doom day-du da doom day-du da da-doom

Dah-doom dah-doom-dah-doom day-du da doom day-du da da-doom-doom!

Never would've thought I'd ever see the day you'd turn away-ay.

Thinking, as I watch you close the final chapters of the page.

People all around are hoping maybe answers you would find.

Little did we know that you were gonna leave us all behind!

Children use their eyes to analyse and learn from what you teach.
(You already know the way I live my life I seldom preach).

But I stand my ground and represent the person that I am,
...So that every day through me you'll see someone who gives damn!

Seeing where you are, yet knowing where you're from is something else!

Hundreds led the way, and thousands lost their lives and gave themselves.

Tryna make a change so each of us appreciate the 'now.

I don't wanna judge but where there is no love we wonder how?

Dah-doom dah-doom-dah-doom day-du da doom day-du da da-doom

Dah-doom dah-doom-dah-doom day-du da doom day-du da da-doom

Dah-doom dah-doom-dah-doom day-du da doom day-du da da-doom

Dah-doom dah-doom-dah-doom day-du da doom day-du da da-doom-doom!

'I WRITE'

I write

...For the rite to do so, / new growth, new heights, /
For the fight in the dog as well as the bite-bark, / Bright
spark, making my mark steps embark, half-mara runner, /
Lycra black swish tick, kits sunners - Winter - Summer / No
looking back on each reach for that medal / Foot down
metaphorical pedal...I write

...For Heavy Metal, Jazz Soul Folk - chokers who smoke, /
Governments that run joke medalling, (in medicines
regardless of your melanin) / To immunise jeopardise plus
manipulate (wait - why?) / Terrorise as they're telling lies
about an antidote, that's even WITH your vote, / Is the very
very reason why ...

I wrote

...This for bitches, witches, warlocks bald heads dreadlocks
in snap backs, / Vegans with reason / Celiacs and that / in
fact, those lactose allergic to dairy & fairy Godmothers with
a bond, / Baby Father's getting it wrong and especially those
getting right!

Yes I write

Mainly just to express, from that place within my chest,
where some only see breast right and left. / For the Amazon
Warrior's quest and Angelina success

And yes... I write

In the night, werewolf's twilight and for the blind man's
insightful wisdom! / Those with freewill still mentally

imprisoned, / Brisbane or Neason of cause you are ALL the very reason!

I write

For the silent, the violent excuses, / Multiple people-users (you know exactly who you is!), / I write like an Erykah sequel on-and-on so, / Flammable droplets to an alky's liver / each tear delivered shimmers shivering in the Sun and sweating in the snow, / 'bout the things you need to know! / I grow in this learning - turning to pen plus rotating from the wrist …like this…

I write this

Ignite just to recite this! / I write for the voiceless, choice-less and aloof, / Scientifically specifically I experiment as living proof / I write through out the rain sunshine and winds whirling, / I write with endorphins for love makers with toes curling / A yearning that makes me write for lives lost priceless at no cost, justice and bad cops / If I eat my words, 'I de write chop'

… and it don't stop…

AMA*Zen*
= **Amazed** with **Zen**

'AMAZED'

We used to laugh and makes joke with each other.
Not at-all like a brother,
More like a pre-mature lover (somewhat undercover)

We both knew it was there,
Just like the folks on 'Big Brother'
...I cannot wait until he meets my 'Mommy!'

His figures ILL like TOMMY!
Alright sorry about the cheesy line ignore me
('cos I'll ignore you when I'm chilling with him!).
I get mixed up like the Lemon - Tonic the 'Juice & 'Gin-Seng'
(sheesh!),
Oh my good-grief-days-and-life "...I'll be your wife!"

So secure about the trust we made,
I'll let Halle Berry come and be our bridesmaid!
Taye Diggs & Tyrese can set our honeymoon suite,
...roses thrown upon the silk sheets now (ya-get-me?!)

You can 'Beyoncé' straight past my fiancée
(ya-hear me?) It's all truth standard!
No nothing else is 'gwaarning.'
My man is 'rugged and raw',
meanwhile he's 'sensitive and charming.'

Arm in arm in love with you,
...although it sounds kinda 'passive' on this beat from Drew
- that goes

bassline ....
....(Pause for thought).

He's second to naught
His game is played, as set and match

I'm 'center court' – (cool)
We're having fun without the rules y'all - sweet
I'm feeling free - he's loving me!
His best friend told him of the love that 'I' felt,
I didn't know myself,
(it's funny when you see what cards are dealt)

My words are true,
It's not to make your hearts melt down.
I…I… feel him now even though he's not around.

I don't care who waits,
Don't care who's bate,
I won't say it's fate…(but it's great!)
I'm frustrated…I waited (for you) …

All my life. All my days.
All my life. All my days.

(Ohh my life! Ohh my days!)
All my life! All my days!

All my life. All my days.
(Ohh my life! Ohh my days!)

All my li-ife… All my day-ays.
All my life. All my days (amazed!)

Some days we kiss and it's like "woah what's this?"
Some other nights it's like… 'alright… alright-alright'
…And then we step back a little.

Sometimes are rocky like skittles,
maybe my Soul and Spirit wants to settle down
… soon enough.
Sometimes are rough and tough – (but I won't cuss),
…'cos seeing and being with him everyday is not enough -
trust me!
We've even private stupid jokes "you're wufferley" and

"stalker-boombyay!"

It means nothing to you,
but we'll be laughing here for three days,
…Freeways, coaches, buses, planes - it's insane,
cos I can never be bored at 'my man' saying 'my name'
To you it's lame, tame, "raah LyricL no shame?"

"…What?"

I'm not hating on what people got but…'What?'
Right now I'm happy now - full stop – 'and what?'

Laying this track is like a feeling shared,
Maybe compared
…Extraordinary - very deep and …'rare-rare'.

I don't care who waits,
Don't care who's bate,
I won't say it's fate…(but it's great!)
I'm frustrated…I waited (for you) …

All my life. All my days.
All my life. All my days.

(Ohh my life! Ohh my days!)
All my life! All my days!

All my life. All my days.
(Ohh my life! Ohh my days!)

All my li-ife... All my day-ays.
All my life. All my days (amazed!)

We fell in love long before we even met
But we both knew the realism still hadn't set in.

Fretting.

I won't forget him in a hurry
(eating a McFlurry....burning it off in a jiffy) Nifty.
Because we're growing older swiftly - Shifty.
Maybe we'll split up when we're like fifty
...Or sixty
...Or seventy-two?
(these times it's probably 'all because of you!')
Until then,
...I'm giving thanks to you - my 'best friend'

My last request is that we manifest and invest in - to our future!

"Yeah a wife and kids will suit-ya - twins
...Possibly girls and later on a baby-bro,
...In like a yellow baby-grow
called 'Udo' or 'Uzo'
(...yeah u know it has to be 'Igbo')"

"Lee - Leo...or Theo?
...And he'll be like our 'Mini-Superhero',
a Mini-WE!"

...You see?

The words are flowing easily
...Hun
...Babes!

Lets take this faze,
To the second stage!
So glad we're on the same page!

There's nothing that I'll even change

Or even try to rearrange!

I don't care who waits,
Don't care who's bate,

I won't say it's fate...(but it's great!)

I'm frustrated
...I waited (for you) ...

All my life. All my days.
All my life. All my days.

(Ohh my life! Ohh my days!)
All my life! All my days!

All my life. All my days.
(Ohh my life! Ohh my days!)

All my li-ife... All my day-ays.
All my life. All my days (amazed!)

'HOW?'

*How do you actually feel about the...way that
I...please?...cos clearly I'm gonna have to break it
down...'cos you're not even...entertaining...what I'm
trying...It's just...gonna break this right the way...)

How?
How? (ow-ow-ow yeah it hurts)

How do you feel about the way that I feel about the way that
YOU feel about the way that I...?

Okay so yeah now I'm crying,
Like Grecian 2000 I be 'dyeing'
...Inside - steady taken for a ride – mistaken.

Taking my weakness in for a kindness,
Meanwhile my love for you was causing blindness
...Because I treated you the finest!

Respected - Interjected
Always on my mind and not neglected
... Perfected,
Talking with our minds and then our spines
... erected.
Standing back to back with fingers linking,
As we're sinking into ...deeper deeper love
...but...

"...Are you ready for us?"
Talking daily we kiss,
But still there's nothing to discuss?
Diss..
Cuss..
(Yep sounds like us),
Living in the past like a Stegosaurus,
...Ignore us when you see us holding hands,

It's just another visual implication of me 'the Girl' and that's
my 'Man!'

I wrote this track - but some say its revealing, (true)
The long and short is I'm at one with my feelings that
everyday you're stealing but...
'how do you feel about the way I feel?'

Or maybe I'm just making it up like its some 'big deal?'
Or maybe when you said 'I love you' then it wasn't real?
"Yeah baby answer that so I can test your skills!" (Chill)

"We can work it out. Where there is a way there's a will"
Loving you ain't some 'role' I play
'Cos it keeps me happy day to day (day-to-day)
Helping me up on my way
...On my way-ay!

How? How?
How do you feel about the way I feel? How?
(ow-ow-ow yeah it hurts)

How? (ow-ow-ow yeah it hurts)
How? (ow-ow-ow yeah it hurts)

How do you feel about the way that I feel about the way that
YOU feel about the way that I...?

Sitting opposite you looking into your eyes at myself

...And then you blink (Blink)
Pick up my drink and then I start to think,
"...Are we really ready to link or even interlink?"

If far 'apart' am I jinxed?
Can we make it alone on our own or do we sink?
I dream about us married sipping champagne
(clink – fizz)
"...'cos baby you're my bizz

And if I had one wish I wouldn't change this!"

Just rearrange this to something splendid that ended,
(Comprehend it?) You sent it,
…Too far away and nearly out of reach,
If life is love then 'here's' the message that I teach,
… I preach
…What I practice,
Plus I ain't no actress the fact is,
(well you get my point just like a cactus)

When we're together then it's (time to flow),
If we're apart then in my heart you'll know it's
(time to grow!)

("Nuh but all jokes aside … and seriously, there is
something there like…and you know this and I know …its
like… you know like a butterscotch schnapps sweetness in
your belly…when the butterflies turn into marshmallow
clouds…just by him looking at me and me touching his
cheek or his chin for a week or maybe fifty two…a whole
year of me and you..it's like…it's all good, it's good!)

How do you feel about the way that I feel about the way that
YOU feel about the way that I…?

'2 BE'

Know how it goes… Know how it feels…
Know how it seems … Know in my dreams …
I know what it feels like,
…To be!

Know how it goes… Know how it feels…
Know how it seems … Know in my dreams …
I know what it feels like,
…To be

I know how it goes when its like, 'yep that's it!'
When you get perplexed and vexed down to your stomach pit,
..crying and sh*t
You can't even spit,
…much less feeling distressed and so far from 'blessed'
…Yes I know!

Peace and quiet you implore,
…Thirty-four new messages,
Six missed calls,
Voicemail
…and now the door! (a'war!)
I know cos I've been there before,
Trying to be nice – yes
…meanwhile still trying to ignore you!

(Yet you have time to talk?)

Linking up with me at half three for Green Tea….yes …And a walk!

Fork out my mouth,
Left jallof on my tongue,
"Haven't come to see me have you?" (and that's just my Mum!)

Learning new things plus upgrading the old,
Wearing my head-wrap and hat on road yet still catching cold?

Pushing the hustle hard - no regrets!
"raaah - what you're still on that music ting?" (y'eedjet!)

Haven't even seen the best of me, don't threat.
'Horses for courses',
...So 'May The Force Be With You',
Laugh the last laugh (ah haa!)

So as the haters forgive!
... Pace yourself
... Tortoise and the hare,
Right time and right place is right here....so just be!

Know how it goes... Know how it feels...
Know how it seems ... Know in my dreams ...
I know what it feels like,
...To be!

Know how it goes... Know how it feels...
Know how it seems ... Know in my dreams ...
I know what it feels like,
...To be

'INNIT?'

Oi! You wanna track with 'ta-cat' in it?
You wanna a tune with 'kaboom' don't it?
You wanna 'rraa-rraa' is it not?
…You want ALL of the above 'cos you Love HipHop, innit?

You wanna track with 'ta-cat' in it?
You wanna a tune with 'kaboom' don't it?
You wanna 'rraa-rraa' is it not?
…You want ALL of the above 'cos you Love HipHop, innit?

I don't really care who cares,
Yuh make them step like stairs,
… Who wins or dares cuts their eyes or stares,
… Vision impaired - you're scared,
Like having nightmares on Elm Street,
…With the tight Breh's that L meets,
…biting air with our ill speech - plus …

HipHop is alive, it's in us,
Stop cuss, your eyes are red,
Watch the ride - I'm your bus,
….er…stop.

Really nearly got this shh on lock …
…or down,
Whether in my jeans or in a frock
…or gown!

The message I send them,
..Will then propel them – (I'll tell them!)
"you better fill them and sell them"
…The track will fill them with venom
(but never kill them…why?)

"…'cos it's not nice."

…But the next emcee will do it too…?

"…but still, its not right!"

Finish.

This is how I flow when I'm in it,

Limit!

…Sixteen bars now - not a minute,

Nip-it!

So the DJ's them will spin it?

Kill it!

…So now you've got your track bruv innit?

Oi! You wanna track with 'ta-cat' in it?
You wanna a tune with 'kaboom' don't it?
You wanna 'rrraa-rraa' is it not?
…you want ALL of the above 'cos you Love HipHop, innit?

'SO FAR (THIS WORLD)'

I'll get to know you-oo
You'll get to know me…and
We'll get to make it so…
So far from this world.

I'll get to know you-oo
You'll get to know me…and
We'll get to make it so…
So far from this world.

Sitting on black sands,
Understand how and why we met,

…As you,
Mesmerise with your eyes, I tend to forget myself.

I now …
know that
it's real!
Smiling to myself – inside

Your full lips,
Igbo hips
…and my loose lips,
Our remix - two souls,
Two souls, (two souls)

We sail (we sail)
We sail (we sail)
…sail – away!

I'll get to know you-oo
You'll get to know me…and
We'll get to make it so…
So far from this world.

I'll get to know you-oo
You'll get to know me...and
We'll get to make it so...
So far from this world.

Heavy now,
Ready now?
Steady now!
...oooo feels so good.

Good enough to eat - sweet enough to... (hmmm!)

We both know,
...we'll both grow

To show
...how revealing - we're feeling.

I've never been so fanatical,
Never been so dramatically,
Compatible and flatter me
...that's with your inner self!

Further along down this avenue,
My attention is grabbing you
Amber perfume I'm double dabbing behind my ear yeah.

Although I saw you pursuing
Didn't know what we were doing,
...brewing – (I should've fallen where I fell?)

I got scared of the notion
while you were talking devotion
"what if we sink like the ocean?"
...but no
You knew we'd sail.

Sail.

You knew we'd sail!

Pass passers by who,

Tried,

Lied and died inside

...'cos they just...
...just didn't know how to love you,
...they didn't know how to
...love you.

...they just
Didn't know.

I'll get to know you-oo
You'll get to know me...and
We'll get to make it so...
So far from this world.

I'll get to know you-oo
You'll get to know me...and
We'll get to make it so...
So far from this world.

_____

'COLD FEET'

Visualizing without compromise.
The essence of you,
Surround the thoughts of me,
...back to the physical of you.

Sprinkled with the insignificant parts I memorize and
call...great!

...Because I'm now waking up.
Facing the pillow which carried your dreams and
"Relaxed your mind"
...And supported your mental journey,
on the night that you said,

...'I...love...you!'

And then became shocked by the sounds of the words,

...someone said with your voice and pronounced with your
lips and relayed with your voice to depict the script he flips
to switch...
To a man who won't admit,
(Who thought it 'would've been me who said it first)

Not reversed
Not pre-rehearsed
...Our feelings just burst into,
8 letter
3 words
...and 2 spaces

Talking but not looking into faces,
(efforts are wasted)
I'm say nothing (now you're now talking for no reason)
Holding the match that sparked,
Evidence of treason.

The season of good will
(Yep this season is good still!)

My will kisses the mouth of my Man from South to stop
talking,

So now our minds are spiritually 'Walking On By' like Syble,
...my middle is queasy
Still feeling uneasy,
...he stops this to squeeze me and ask me if
"I love he...?"

(Damn, this sh1ts never easy!)

I'm looking at when we first met,
...to when I first got wet,
...to when he first got upset,
...to when his ex was a threat!

The disposition in my intuition
"Could never get back into her old position" (I just listened)

The dances.
The holding.
The never scalding,
Understanding.
Physical parts are so demanding.
The walks - The talks - Quality – "Mine All Mine"

Our planets out of line..?
(...in good time!)

I had mine.
Sisters would rave and talk and go shopping,
...its not stopping its moving improving and soothing,
Kisses on my forehead with eyes closed.
Soft lips like a rose to the senses,
Dimensions. (We intertwine like extensions)
We mix well and keep the spice like Jamaican Ginger Cake!

Hot oven love is the love that we bake,
We make,
His snake in my grasp,
I escaped from his clasp,
...it's something worth holding...?

(Ignoring the clothes that you're folding)

Ignoring the future we were moulding,
The pictures of you and me kissing the Spalding

The Silence is Golden,

My heart if frozen,
... emptiness like the Ozone,

My onyx is shattered,
...and now the only thing that matters is...

"THE MATRIX DVD
YOU ARE REACHING FOR ...
EASILY ...
HAPPENS ...
TO BELONG ...
TO ME!...Baaaby...!?"

So now that's where we be.

There's no 'me and he'
I haven't finish...so (shh)... nuh-budda "shhh" me
....I'm still talking!

I love you yet you're still walking
...out of my life,
my house,
my feelings,
my heart ...minor
(...you've test driven my vagina!?)

In life appreciate the finer things,

Like the days when the 'heart sings',
Brings to mind that I LOVE YOU!
(...although I haven't 'said it')
...Though in my eyes you read it.

But now You cut ...
And edit
And eject
And neglect our Utopia..?

So now I'm just scoping yah

Me ...coping? Yeah...
...cos I knew you would leave,

If I loved you, would you believe?
Meet some chick with a weave?
Meet some trick with no sleeves?
Meet Dick and roll leaves and weed in Battersea?
(I couldn't stay for the tragedy!)

But gradually I felt at one with you - casually.

Imagine me,
...so glad that every day you badger me!

(Getting 'aggie')

The play-off dunk that's a 'backy'

Before, 'Salt-fish & Ackee'

'Soup & Shakky'

'Chris Tucker and Jackie'...

..but now
But now the picture's looking tacky!

Either I tell you - then you'd leave,
Think I'm lying disbelieve,
Tell me I'm naïve…
(oh please) ….

…Come home!

Where the heart is,

…And where my heart is,

…Or where your heart used to be,

Its still bad news to me,
Like NYC
…My Man has Traded his…

World
Centre

…Me.

Upgraded
Now hands free
No talk time and definitely
No credit (I didn't beg it, I said it!)

And if I asked you,
…Would - you – blast?
…Kiss your teeth and walk past?
…Our last - few - moments lasting longer.

(Allow the dwelling - because there's nothing left worth
telling!)

When you're 'phoning'

I'm moaning
Getting vexed
With your 'texts'
I'm no better with your 'letter',
...and your 'email' ...oh well!

You know you're just a 'bro who had to go',
...although...

It took a long time...but..

...Now we're talking!

Holding hands while we're walking!
Chest to chests
Hearts beating!
We're saying things without *speaking*!

Flavour...
Behaviour...
So sweet so we savour ahhh
There's no more Cold Feet...

There's no more...

...so to speak.

'TO ME ME'

I feel super-duper fantabulous - miraculous!
Happiness sprinkled on top and there I'll pop a cherry-
berry.

Yes indeed it's so necessary
...to give thanks and smile for amazing things that everyday
brings like,

When the birds sings in the spring
And the bees hum in the summer
(though we fought them last autumn),
Winter comes round and the sky-like ground
is all white,
True you're inside, everything alright!

Safe warm,
Padded up like sweetcorn
A new year,
New born,
New beginnings and plus you're winning!

Spinning the world on your fingertips
...new trips,
Clothes that fit your hips,
Champagne sips like 'ahh!' (ahh!)

It's all great, new friends meeting pals and mates,
Baking cakes,
Picnic at the Lake District.

Couple of cans in Cannes,
Teppanyaki in Japan,
Head back arms span its like damn...I'm happs!!

Rap when I wanna sing, then I wanna dance, when I'm in
your arms,

cos I think about you.

Spit when I wanna rap,
Then I wanna rhyme,
Then I wanna sing,
'cos I'm doing my thing.

Roll when I wanna flow,
Spit a little rhyme every single time,
'cos you make me smile smile.

These are the things that you
...do do do, do, do-do-dooo
To me me me, meeee

These are the things that you do do do.
To me me meee, me, me, mee-e.

Then they'ld be saying like,
"Oi? Have you won the lottery or suttin'?"
I'm like, "naah man, just had some nice Curry Mutton!"

Macaroni cheese, salad, avocado,
Tomato near the middle,
(then I used to be too 'brock' to go to Lidl!)

Even too poor for the £1 Store?
'cos every month I paid a bill
Another month they wanted more
...still and more
hat a war,
Couldn't ignore the fact I kept feeling low,

Until I let it all go!
To grow and succeed with the plant or seed of prayer,
I wasn't afraid to try,
(Just a little scared)

Everything changed rearrange for the better,

Wrote a sonnet type, singing rapping style kinda letter, …To myself!
What I want to happen
Took myself seriously,
…So that I wasn't just chatting.

I actually felt from the letters that I spelt - love for self,
The plus point was wealth and health - Believe!

Rap when I wanna sing, then I wanna dance, when I'm in your arms,
cos I think about you.

Spit when I wanna rap,
Then I wanna rhyme,
Then I wanna sing,
'cos I'm doing my thing.

Roll when I wanna flow,
Spit a little rhyme every single time,
'cos you make me smile smile.

These are the things that you
…do do do, do, do-do-dooo
To me me me, meeee

These are the things that you do do do.
To me me meee, me, me, mee-e.

'HIGHER'

Higher
Higher

Getting up, high - higher
It's all about getting up higher! Much
No much higher than that, much higher in fact.
Keep getting up!

Getting up, high - higher
It's all about getting up higher! Much
No much higher than that, much higher in fact.
Keep getting up!

Higher than expected.
Feeling slightly sceptic.
Except the fact that there's no limits,
No fake eyelash fat titty 'gimmicks' cynics
…or pretty-boy pin-ups to pin this,
Pin back your lobes, 'Beyonce-J-Lo bottom's, (hail no!)

So lets deal with this, bare-face realness.
…'cos if I don't like you,
Then my music won't excite you
…then I straight won't invite you!
Stops people losing! Stops all confusing!
(Stops your eye and top-lip dem from bruising!)

Refusing the fact there's none for messing,
Second guessing. Saying what I feel, because the music has a
message, listen….(listen….ooow!)

Passing the baton, 'Lioness' with finesse?
…or are you just 'pussy' type chat chatting?
(Help where it's needed)
Feed how you were fed
('Miss Lead' are you sinking?)

103

Well here's an easy question if you like
'whatcha drinking?'

I'm thinking your five year plans my 'weak one!'
To work out where I'm going - look far back where I begun
…and then how?
…and then pow
…you're right there, the right footing!

Criticising easy when you have no real 'beginning',
…or look in,
just a bring in, the thing is
I feel it deep within my marrow,
…With eyes of hawk!
(Watching the pigeon kinda sparrows)
That night owl even …in the day!

You're sleeping on this vessel
That's all, (yes I've said it!)
Point is now is imbedded,
Marinate until you get it
And don't hate or you'll regret it, y'get me?
('Cos me, I kinda get in where I fit in)

But please don't think I'm smug,
I'm just a teeny bitty smitten.

I inspire, with a tightrope schedule,
On tight rope wire,
Give thanks to The Father 'cos the Devil is liar,
Hold tight to your desires
Just to keep it much higher
… Getting up!

Getting up, high - higher
It's all about getting up higher! Much
No much higher than that, much higher in fact.
Keep getting up!

Getting up, high - higher
It's all about getting up higher! Much
No much higher than that, much higher in fact.
Keep getting up!

No no, there's No 'i' in team,
Because my eyes are on the dream.
Focused on the plan,
Supply demand
Commands the gift of over-standing.

Making a difference where there isn't,
Using everything you have as well as Wisdom
(No no, not talking 'Dental')

Drop an instrument
And its far from accidental or happenstance.
I'll have a dance
Calamari? DimSum?

Take a risk or even bring some,
You never know you'll maybe grow some,
…or know someone who used to own some?

But hay (Hay!)
What can I say - there's none for playing!
I know what I mean,
plus mean exactly every word I'm saying.

Staying in a mode that's far from set and stone,
Moving out of your 'City',
…is little little bit like moving home.

Foundation.

Where it started.

…'cos home is where the heart is,

So you must proceed,
At least depart where you departed.

Breaking eggs,
Taking risks,
Shake-a-leg,
Take a miss'ion,
Shaking hands,
Pounding fists,
(ok, you finishing packing?)

…You're saying 'eerr dunno..?',
Then there's something you're lacking!
So then go back in and then be ready
…once you're ready!
Atlas on it axis keeps continuously spinning,
Now go ahead and stick your pin in,

…Nothing left to do but winning.
Keep it high!

Getting up, high - higher
It's all about getting up higher! Much
No much higher than that, much higher in fact.
Keep getting up!

Getting up, high - higher
It's all about getting up higher! Much
No much higher than that, much higher in fact.
Keep getting up!

'AWAY'

I took myself away.
I took my – self…away.
I took myself away – from you!

I took myself away.
I took my – self…away.
I took myself away – from you!

I took my size 7½'s to 8,
… out of my mouth

I took my
….can't stop interrupting, when your talking its erupting.

I took my,
Doubting what you're saying,
And then showing me something else?

… self

…Away!

I took my
….insecure but secure enough to read your text's from your
ex's,
…it vexes me but I… I had to!

Take my …

"eenuh!, "why you all up inna-my business?",

What is this? (Mannn!)

I had to take myself away!

I took myself away.

I took my – self…away.
I took myself away – from you!

I took myself away.
I took my – self…away.
I took myself away – from you!

I took my, (my),
'My' section of the joint account out,
…just to prove that 'I' too "could amount
… to nothing!" Yeah!

Oh and, I took my "run-up-my-gums" to my Mum's.
I took my screaming at your lies and puffy red eyes far far!

I took my gullible or naive, (edit what I wanna believe!)
Whilst keeping the "L, I love you… please?!…"
"…baby don't go…. so-what …you're just gonna leave?"
Looking up at me from your knees,
Whilst making me Wonder like 'Steve' (ohhh pleease!?)

I took my size 12-14 into a size 8-10
…and then back again!
I took my mobile number and changed it to…
 … 2…different post codes zones or modes,
…to somewhere hot … from somewhere cold
(Yes I was that ***ing bold!)

I took my …

…. self AWAY!

'ALWAYS ALWAYS'

Boom-boom bah boompah - Boom-boom bah boompah
Boom-boom bah boompah - Boom-boom bah boompah

So open minded,
So true and kind
It's so hard to find these days

Caring and just,
Someone to trust,
It so is a must he stays,

Intelligent too,
Sexy and yet cute,
Music - guess who?...he plays!

Of course he can cook and whine down to Zouk,
...so don't get it shook always yeah!

So open minded,
So true and kind
It's so hard to find these days

Caring and just,
Someone to trust,
It so is a must he stays,

Intelligent too,
Sexy and yet cute,
Music - guess who?...he plays!

Of course he can cook and whine down to Zouk,
...so don't get it shook always yeah!

It's like a super surprise,
Mesmerized - hypnotised
... Plus that look in your eyes,

109

(I mean keen!)

When I'm holding your hand,
I just don't understand at all,
… furthermore he's so tall,

Plus with a beautiful face,
What I thought was a 'King of Jacks',
…in fact's an 'Ace of Hearts'
Start
…As I mean to go on,
What I feel's really strong
…so I'm putting this song to you boo
Always!

Whenever you need me,
I'll be there.

Whenever you call,
I'll answer to you…

Always
Always
Always - Always

Whenever you need me,
I'll be there.

Whenever you call,
I'll answer to you…

Always
Always
Always - Always
Boom-boom bah boompah - Boom-boom bah boompah
Boom-boom bah boompah - Boom-boom bah boompah

Really couldn't resist,
'What is this?'

'Whadda deal?'
'Is it real?',
Make a wish or just pray.

Kinda happened like that,
Not like a secret attack,
...more like a magical hat and then ...bam!
(...that's with an alakazam)

Into your arms I ran,
Anything for this man,
I will do!

True. To bone - never leave him alone,
...'cos what I feel's 'so at home',
That's with you...always.

Whenever you need me,
I'll be there.

Whenever you call,
I'll answer to you...

Always
Always
Always - Always

Boom-boom bah boompah - Boom-boom bah boompah
Boom-boom bah boompah - Boom-boom bah boompah

'NOW!'

Sign of the times, there no time to waste,
Less haste plus more speed indeed we proceed,
To feed and succeed (in Burbury or Tweed),
Like Keanu Reeves in 'Speed' yes we take lead – plus,

'Forest Gump'ing' this triple jump,
We flip the funk and tip the trunk,
Out sip the drunk ...drink?
(Yo'wassup with this is!)
Ray Charles your 'fat wrist' with no witnesses!

Now - Really (and I mean sincerely),
Mouth watering beats when they seep you're teary,
"I like what you tried to do...yeah nearly,
You're more like 'Jim' as opposed to Mariah Carey yeah..."

I didn't mean to offend,
Comprehend what I'm telling you
I'm a friend-ish...
...This dish - like a delicate lesson,
Sweet feed just to savour this delicatessen!

Now (Now?) See it de?

Baa Baa Baaaa! 'cos you're muttering mutton,
Rapping and fronting ,
Everyday you're doing me suttin' (please – Jeeez!')
But can you 'rock it with ease?'
Shelf-life 'quick-fast' like a Japanese Sneeze.

I'm checking your 'raps'
Checking the stats,
Taking the facts,
You're taking a slap
(Not taking it back),
Who's taking a cab or taxi?

Call a 'Priest' like Maxi,
And come back when you're sick enough to need a vaccine!

Now…

You know you've been undone?
Plus inside you kinda like know where I'm coming from
…right?

Some come shed some light,
Push come to shove,
Don King the fight,
Skills are mad tight … fine.

Take your time.

Although I kinda blaintantly helped
Right there to draw the line.
There's no point from A-to-B,
Unless there's money to make,
decimal point away from me,
…right now!

Now!

_____

'TAKE IT OFF'

I'm feeling whole again!
See how we roll my friend?
…like kinda born again,
I'm semi naked
…naked.

I'm feeling whole again!
See how we roll my friend?
…I'm kind of born again
…I'm semi naked,
Naked.
Take it.
Take it off!
Take it off - yeah,
Take it off! Take it off - yeah!

Come on now –Yuh, woo!
Naked - Naked.
Naked? Take it …take it take it off man,
Chillax and just take it…aawwff??!!

(I'm happy for you!)

I'm happy for you too.
You see we have like two or twenty-two days of Summer in
London,

Give or take the odd rainy rainbow evening
…believe me the morning dew is due to start about
…(what seven?) 07:00 a.m.

The birds singing and its simply – beautiful!
…and when it's … beautiful…

Then there's those guys,
 Wearing those yellow t-shirts,

Women with the lime linen jackets,
… the salmon suits…
That suit the mood of the day,
(and that's just going to work!)
…And that's going to work ,
…'cos it's a good look!

Then you've got those dog walkers,
The talkers,
Joggers in jogging bottoms and shorts,

Sizes that mesmerize the eyes,
Thick thighs,
…just be yourself maaaan!

You only live one life!,
…so you may as well live it,
…with bright colours like a peacock dancing to the
'Rainbow' theme tune,
"…paint the whole world…"
Whatever man!

But seriously, the shape of things to come,
… comes to mind!

Come eight o'clock the Moon replaces the luminous shoe
laces,
Matching footless tights,
…its alright!

Open toe shoes,
Base ball caps and Bar-b-que's,
Fruit stalls,
Buying strawberries – yes please?
B-ball court and all sorts,
… (and all dem tings),
That's just one freak Sunny day of Spring!
(whatta-ting!)

…But seriously - seriously

We have different skin types that delight,
Golden Brown,
Black and White,

Hair shades ,
Multiple colours,
Weaves and braids
…And grade one fades.

(Then there's those pretty boys with the bald-heads like
Morris Chestnut)
"I'll call you?'"
I guess not …
…And what?

Walking along the Waterloo,
Not as in 'Nelson' or 'ABBA' but the Thames!

The 'London Eye' will grab your attention span,
Not to mention the 'African Man' - Percussionist,
Cyclist,
B-boys and girls spinning on their wrists,
Water-fights…water pisssssstol's,
Folding paper-fans,

…So now you understand.
Why I'm semi …naked
…Naked…take it… take it… take it…

Take it off.

'SWEET YOU'

I hope this'll sweet you.

Just enough to make you smile,

a little while so you and I will feel oh so good.

I hope this'll sweet you.

So baby maybe,
Take a little time I know your mine and you and I will be cool

I hope this'll sweet you.

Just enough to make you smile, a little while so you and I will feel oh so good.

I hope this'll sweet you.

Baby maybe, take a little time
I know your mine and you and I will be cool

I hope this - so hold this - notice my - feelings
I hope this - quote this - wrote this with meaning
… feeling you

Its essential to be sensual
When it's a sensitive matter of this kind.

Burning frankincense incense that sends intense cents
That spends…
Time
…in the air.

Which twists and turns in turn so as to move your senses
Without being sensible enough to know,

What to do with that very feeling.

Judging by this very sentence, its intense contents and what it represents as a multi-sense,

... I

... try

To decipher.

You.

Kinda like ...err I don't know,
Using my spidey-senses, (to the senseless few),
Who knew not what you did, but what you do
...to me.

Your very existence and presence,
Presents an omnipotence of happiness.

And for that...

...I hope this'll sweet you!

I hope this - so hold this - notice my - feelings
I hope this - quote this - wrote this with meaning
... feeling you

I hope this'll sweet you.

Just enough to make you smile,

a little while so you and I will feel oh so good.

I hope this'll sweet you.

So baby maybe,
Take a little time I know your mine and you and I will be cool

I hope this'll sweet you.

Just enough to make you smile, a little while so you and I will feel oh so good.

I hope this'll sweet you.

Baby maybe, take a little time
I know your mine and you and I will be cool

_____

AMA*Zen*
= **Amazed** with **Zen**

About The Author:
Lyricist, Singer-Songwriter, Emcee (MC), Spokenword BEFFTA
Award Winner 2014 and Artist-Tutor LyricL, is a jubilant, exultant
performer, whose animated fresh style exudes joy, in a euphoric
and beautiful way!
LyricL lights up mics and stages with her performances. Her
eclectic catalogue spans Hip-Hop, House, Jazz through to Afro and
Broken Beat with a soulful edge, stirring grooves enhanced by her
lyricism and Spokenword. Born in London to Nigerian parents,
LyricL's early and enduring musical influences came from home.
A drummer/DJ Daddy, who loved African Jazz, Gospel and High
Life, entertained with chest-tap percussion, beatbox, whilst
skillfully playing his hands as wind instruments, as Master Chef
Mommy dances and sings in her own key of happiness, to this very
day. That vibe and energy continues throughout her current works.
Unapologetic originality, lyrical dexterity and openness to
innovate, elate and debate.

Acknowledgments
Give Thanks To The Almighty Merciful, All-Powerful, Insightful
Delightful Creator that created us *Creatives* into being! Being
thankful for love, life, learning, living and giving from that space
which needs to be nurtured and inspired daily in order to actually
write, recite, share and creatively *care* in general.

The Father, My Father, Moses M.O.M, My "Sweet Modda"
(Mommy Juliet) J Double, The Twins (however balance or
unbalance that love is), My little big Brother Obi. God Father A,
GodSon Ahmir & God Daughter Cariosa. (You are both winners!)
my beloved Nieces, Nephews, Cousins and sub-cousins (the ones
whose folks we CALL Aunty) I thanks and love unequivocally.
Cousin Felix…"lenu book!"

My Music Family who have shown support on and off stage, in

and out of the booth, Infront of the scene and sincerely and consistently behind the scene (and my back,) yes indeed, it is all love. The writers whose verses made 'Amazed' amazing as guest features including Paul, Log!c, Motet, Pesci, Sarina, Enrico, JoLeon, Heidi, BabySol, Kevin MT. The producers, DJ's and musicians that inspired me to do more Drew, Daz, Andre, Zulu, Spinna, Mashi and my extended Muso family who kept the fire vibrant with warmth and positivity, asking me to later feature on songs and stages in countries I would have never ever expected to see, visit or share which helped me to get to where I am now ever after my Pop's and many loved ones transitioned, you were indeed light, without even knowing it.

The humbling in seeing people with less doing more in continents sharing context, content and compassion. The Creative Organisations, Humanitarian Charities and Educators who permitted me to teach what I too was experientially taught, in order to see people blossom, mentor, facilitate and creative awareness, life skills, heART and therapy, all through spokenword.

To the industry professionals who see and believe in opportunity, overlook as well as embrace everything and everyone outside of the conventional boxes of thought. I acknowledge you too. To the pure and close relationships, relationSHITs, friendships, sports-wo/manships, Penmanships, Artistics Artists, Dancers, Writers, Poets, Musicians, Chai Chat time-makers, Two cheek kissers, huggers that show love who I see regularly and don't know …but actually do. Those who I hold dear who selflessly give me feedback, texts, calls, emails, comments online and one-to-one moments. The most valuable thing you have given to me even now, is your time. This we cannot get back but we can capture it's richness.

In the stillness of my inner self, the prompter of my Soul, with all that I am and all that I hold dear, I appreshelove, adore and thank you for just for coming along this journey. It may have been what you expected or perhaps not, either way, it still is… **AmaZEN**.

Lightning Source UK Ltd.
Milton Keynes UK
UKOW04f0624261017
311677UK00001B/75/P